IN ASSOCIATION WITH

SQA

Hodder Gibson
Model Practice
Papers
WITH ANSWERS

PLUS: Official SQA Specimen Paper &
2014 Past Paper With Answers

National 5
Design &
Manufacture

2013 Specimen Question Paper,
Model Papers & 2014 Exam

COMPANY

This book contains the official 2013 SQA Specimen Question Paper and 2014 Exam for National 5 Design and Manufacture, with associated SQA approved answers modified from the official marking instructions that accompany the paper.

In addition the book contains model practice papers, together with answers, plus study skills advice. These papers, some of which may include a limited number of previously published SQA questions, have been specially commissioned by Hodder Gibson, and have been written by experienced senior teachers and examiners in line with the new National 5 syllabus and assessment outlines, Spring 2013. This is not SQA material but has been devised to provide further practice for National 5 examinations in 2014 and beyond.

Hodder Gibson is grateful to the copyright holders, as credited on the final page of the Answer Section, for permission to use their material. Every effort has been made to trace the copyright holders and to obtain their permission for the use of copyright material. Hodder Gibson will be happy to receive information allowing us to rectify any error or omission in future editions.

Hachette UK's policy is to use papers that are natural, renewable and recyclable products and made from wood grown in sustainable forests. The logging and manufacturing processes are expected to conform to the environmental regulations of the country of origin.

Orders: please contact Bookpoint Ltd, 130 Park Drive, Abingdon, Oxon OX14 4SE. Telephone: (44) 01235 827720. Fax: (44) 01235 400454. Lines are open 9.00–5.00, Monday to Saturday, with a 24-hour message answering service. Visit our website at www.hoddereducation.co.uk. Hodder Gibson can be contacted direct on: Tel: 0141 848 1609; Fax: 0141 889 6315; email: hoddergibson@hodder.co.uk

This collection first published in 2014 by
Hodder Gibson, an imprint of Hodder Education,
An Hachette UK Company
2a Christie Street
Paisley PA1 1NB

{BrightRED   Hodder Gibson is grateful to Bright Red Publishing Ltd for collaborative work in preparation of this book and all SQA Past Paper, National 5 and Higher for CfE Model Paper titles 2014.

Typeset by PDQ Digital Media Solutions Ltd, Bungay, Suffolk NR35 1BY

Printed in the UK

A catalogue record for this title is available from the British Library

ISBN: 978-1-4718-3699-2

3 2 1

2015 2014

Introduction

Study Skills – what you need to know to pass exams!

Pause for thought

Many students might skip quickly through a page like this. After all, we all know how to revise. Do you really though?

Think about this:

"IF YOU ALWAYS DO WHAT YOU ALWAYS DO, YOU WILL ALWAYS GET WHAT YOU HAVE ALWAYS GOT."

Do you like the grades you get? Do you want to do better? If you get full marks in your assessment, then that's great! Change nothing! This section is just to help you get that little bit better than you already are.

There are two main parts to the advice on offer here. The first part highlights fairly obvious things but which are also very important. The second part makes suggestions about revision that you might not have thought about but which WILL help you.

Part 1

DOH! It's so obvious but ...

Start revising in good time

Don't leave it until the last minute – this will make you panic.

Make a revision timetable that sets out work time AND play time.

Sleep and eat!

Obvious really, and very helpful. Avoid arguments or stressful things too – even games that wind you up. You need to be fit, awake and focused!

Know your place!

Make sure you know exactly **WHEN and WHERE** your exams are.

Know your enemy!

Make sure you know what to expect in the exam.

How is the paper structured?

How much time is there for each question?

What types of question are involved?

Which topics seem to come up time and time again?

Which topics are your strongest and which are your weakest?

Are all topics compulsory or are there choices?

Learn by DOING!

There is no substitute for past papers and practice papers – they are simply essential! Tackling this collection of papers and answers is exactly the right thing to be doing as your exams approach.

Part 2

People learn in different ways. Some like low light, some bright. Some like early morning, some like evening / night. Some prefer warm, some prefer cold. But everyone uses their BRAIN and the brain works when it is active. Passive learning – sitting gazing at notes – is the most INEFFICIENT way to learn anything. Below you will find tips and ideas for making your revision more effective and maybe even more enjoyable. What follows gets your brain active, and active learning works!

Activity 1 – Stop and review

Step 1

When you have done no more than 5 minutes of revision reading STOP!

Step 2

Write a heading in your own words which sums up the topic you have been revising.

Step 3

Write a summary of what you have revised in no more than two sentences. Don't fool yourself by saying, "I know it, but I cannot put it into words". That just means you don't know it well enough. If you cannot write your summary, revise that section again, knowing that you must write a summary at the end of it. Many of you will have notebooks full of blue/black ink writing. Many of the pages will not be especially attractive or memorable so try to liven them up a bit with colour as you are reviewing and rewriting. **This is a great memory aid, and memory is the most important thing.**

Activity 2 — Use technology!

Why should everything be written down? Have you thought about "mental" maps, diagrams, cartoons and colour to help you learn? And rather than write down notes, why not record your revision material?

What about having a text message revision session with friends? Keep in touch with them to find out how and what they are revising and share ideas and questions.

Why not make a video diary where you tell the camera what you are doing, what you think you have learned and what you still have to do? No one has to see or hear it, but the process of having to organise your thoughts in a formal way to explain something is a very important learning practice.

Be sure to make use of electronic files. You could begin to summarise your class notes. Your typing might be slow, but it will get faster and the typed notes will be easier to read than the scribbles in your class notes. Try to add different fonts and colours to make your work stand out. You can easily Google relevant pictures, cartoons and diagrams which you can copy and paste to make your work more attractive and **MEMORABLE**.

Activity 3 – This is it. Do this and you will know lots!

Step 1

In this task you must be very honest with yourself! Find the SQA syllabus for your subject (www.sqa.org.uk). Look at how it is broken down into main topics called MANDATORY knowledge. That means stuff you MUST know.

Step 2

BEFORE you do ANY revision on this topic, write a list of everything that you already know about the subject. It might be quite a long list but you only need to write it once. It shows you all the information that is already in your long-term memory so you know what parts you do not need to revise!

Step 3

Pick a chapter or section from your book or revision notes. Choose a fairly large section or a whole chapter to get the most out of this activity.

With a buddy, use Skype, Facetime, Twitter or any other communication you have, to play the game "If this is the answer, what is the question?". For example, if you are revising Geography and the answer you provide is "meander", your buddy would have to make up a question like "What is the word that describes a feature of a river where it flows slowly and bends often from side to side?".

Make up 10 "answers" based on the content of the chapter or section you are using. Give this to your buddy to solve while you solve theirs.

Step 4

Construct a wordsearch of at least 10 X 10 squares. You can make it as big as you like but keep it realistic. Work together with a group of friends. Many apps allow you to make wordsearch puzzles online. The words and phrases can go in any direction and phrases can be split. Your puzzle must only contain facts linked to the topic you are revising. Your task is to find 10 bits of information to hide in your puzzle, but you must not repeat information that you used in Step 3. DO NOT show where the words are. Fill up empty squares with random letters. Remember to keep a note of where your answers are hidden but do not show your friends. When you have a complete puzzle, exchange it with a friend to solve each other's puzzle.

Step 5

Now make up 10 questions (not "answers" this time) based on the same chapter used in the previous two tasks. Again, you must find NEW information that you have not yet used. Now it's getting hard to find that new information! Again, give your questions to a friend to answer.

Step 6

As you have been doing the puzzles, your brain has been actively searching for new information. Now write a NEW LIST that contains only the new information you have discovered when doing the puzzles. Your new list is the one to look at repeatedly for short bursts over the next few days. Try to remember more and more of it without looking at it. After a few days, you should be able to add words from your second list to your first list as you increase the information in your long-term memory.

FINALLY! Be inspired...

Make a list of different revision ideas and beside each one write **THINGS I HAVE** tried, **THINGS I WILL** try and **THINGS I MIGHT** try. Don't be scared of trying something new.

And remember – "FAIL TO PREPARE AND PREPARE TO FAIL!"

National 5 Design and Manufacture

The exam

The following guidance will give you a clear plan to take into the examination room and help you achieve better grades. The Design and Manufacture examination is split into two sections.

Section 1

Section 1 is worth 24 marks and will ask questions based around the workshop manufacturing techniques that could be used to manufacture a simple product. All the questions in this section will be about the product and its component parts. It is likely that there will be a mixture of materials used in the manufacture of the product. Those materials will most likely be wood, metal and plastic.

A good examination preparation strategy would be to ensure you have knowledge of the properties of a range of softwoods, hardwoods, ferrous and non-ferrous metals, thermoplastics and thermosetting plastics.

In addition, you will need to be familiar with common workshop processes using these materials. The tools and equipment used with these materials are also areas which you should study. Remember – none of this is new to you and you will have spent time on the Design and Manufacture course making a range of projects from these materials. Be confident.

Section 2

Section 2 is worth 36 marks and will ask questions mainly about the design part of the course, though there will be around 6 marks worth of manufacturing questions, which will ask about manufacturing in industry.

The design questions will come from a range of topics which you will have covered in the course, such as the design team, the design process, design factors, sketching, modelling, product evaluation and specifications.

A simple word can be used to help you remember the design factors: **FEEDSCAMP**

Each letter stands for one of the design factors: **F**unction, **E**rgonomics, **E**nvironmental concerns, **D**urability, **S**afety, **C**ost (economics), **A**esthetics, **M**aterials and **P**roduction.

If you use this as a memory aid, you should be able to answer any question that asks about design factors. There are obviously additional areas contained within these headings, but it is a great help to have one word that reminds you of all the areas.

For the rest of the questions in this section, you should think back through your course and the work you did in the Design Unit. This should help you answer the questions about the design process, sketching, modelling, specifications and the product evaluation activities you were involved with.

Where marks are commonly lost

One of the major problems that markers find is the lack of description in students' answers. When asked about design factors in relation to a given product, such as a kettle, the usual response is:

"The kettle should be safe and durable."

Although this is correct, we could be talking about any product on the planet, for example a watch should also be safe and durable.

To gain full marks, you should make clear reference to the product being asked about, so if we answer again about the kettle, the answer should be:

"It needs to be safe because the body of the kettle could get very hot with the boiling water and you could burn yourself. It needs to be durable because during the lifespan of a kettle it may get banged in the kitchen sink when being filled and it should withstand these collisions."

When you look at the response above you can clearly see that we are talking about a kettle now and not a watch. Try to do this through the whole of the paper, specifically in Section 2 when each question is about a different product.

Another area where candidates answer poorly is within the product evaluation question. You should try to extend your answers to fully describe the activities you would carry out with reference to the product being asked about. Too often responses are simplistic, for example, when being asked about evaluating the ease of use of a vacuum cleaner:

"They should do a user trial."

Or when being asked about value for money of a vacuum cleaner:

"They should do a comparison with other products."

Once again, these answers are correct, but do not explain the activity in any detail and would therefore not attract full marks.

An exemplar answer would be:

"They should carry out a user trial, where a range of users vacuum an area of carpet and then describe how easy or difficult they found the vacuum cleaner to manoeuvre around small items of furniture.

They should look at a range of existing vacuum cleaners that perform similar functions and see what their selling price is. They could then compare the selling price to theirs and this will show if their vacuum cleaner is good value for money."

Where improvements could be made to achieve better grades

If you want to achieve a better grade you should think about the way you answer other questions, such as questions that ask for "properties of materials that make them suitable for a particular product."

If you try to explain the properties of HDPE it may be difficult and the ones you choose may not relate directly to the product being asked about. Try to list the properties the product needs to have to be successful at its function. If we take the example of a milk container made from HDPE, we can then say that HDPE can be recycled, it is available in a range of colours and it is non-toxic. These are all "things" that the milk container does because it is a milk container not because it is made of HDPE. All of your properties of materials questions can be answered this way if you refer to "what the product needs to do" rather than the material.

The ergonomics question is where you could rack up vital extra marks. This question can be answered in lots of ways, but it is a good idea to have a plan before you go into the exam in case the ergonomics question is in the paper.

Think about the three aspects of ergonomics: anthropometrics, physiology and psychology.

Try to write two answers for each area relating to the product in the question.

There is a simple formula to help you get full marks in this question.

For anthropometrics, pick a part of the product and then pick a part of the human body that should fit on/into that part. Link them together in a sentence and you get one mark. Do that twice to get full marks. E.g. Kettle: the handle of the kettle should fit the adult male palm width.

For physiology, pick a part of the product and then come up with a verb that you would do with that part. Link them together in a sentence and you get one mark. Do that twice to get full marks. E.g. Kettle: filling should be easy so the lid should be easy to open.

For psychology, pick a part of the product and then come up with a feeling or emotion to do with that part. Link them together in a sentence and you get one mark. Do that twice to get full marks. E.g. Kettle: the switch on the kettle should make a clicking sound to let you know that it is on.

Good luck!

Remember that the rewards for passing National 5 Design and Manufacture are well worth it! Your pass will help you get the future you want for yourself. In the exam, be confident in your own ability. If you're not sure how to answer a question trust your instincts and just give it a go anyway. Keep calm and don't panic! GOOD LUCK!

2013 Specimen Question Paper

N5

National
Qualifications
SPECIMEN ONLY

Mark

SQ16/N5/01

Design and Manufacture

Date — Not applicable

Duration — 1 hour and 30 minutes

Fill in these boxes and read what is printed below.

Full name of centre

Town

Forename(s)

Surname

Number of seat

Date of birth

Day   Month   Year

D D   M M   Y Y

Scottish candidate number

Total marks — 60

SECTION 1 — 24 marks

Attempt ALL questions.

SECTION 2 — 36 marks

Attempt ALL questions.

Read every question carefully before you attempt it.

Write your answers, clearly in the spaces provided, using **blue** or **black** ink.

Show all working and units where appropriate.

Before leaving the examination room you must give this booklet to the Invigilator.
If you do not, you may lose all the marks for this paper.

MARKS | DO NOT WRITE IN THIS MARGIN

SECTION 1 — 24 marks

Attempt ALL questions

1. A pupil's project for a TV stand and storage unit is shown in the photo below.

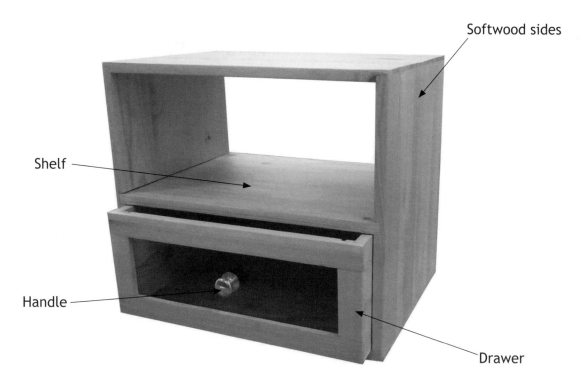

Softwood sides

Shelf

Handle

Drawer

(a) The base of the drawer was constructed from a manufactured board and the sides from softwood.

(i) State the name of a suitable manufactured board for the base of the drawer.

1

(ii) Describe **three** benefits of using a manufactured board for the base of the drawer.

3

MARKS

1. (a) (continued)

(iii) Describe **two** sustainability issues that may have made softwood the preferred material for the sides of the TV stand.

2

_____

_____

_____

(b) The photo below shows the joint in the side of the TV stand used to hold the shelf.

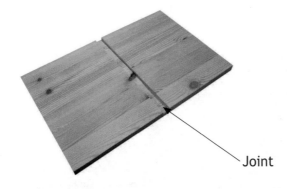

Joint

(i) Give a reason why the joint shown above is suitable.

1

_____

(ii) Describe **three** stages required to manufacture this type of joint using hand tools in a school workshop.

3

_____

_____

_____

_____

(c) Clear varnish was used as a surface finish for the softwood.

(i) Describe **two** benefits of using clear varnish as a surface finish for the softwood.

2

_____

_____

1. (c) (continued)

    (ii) Describe **two** stages in the preparation of the softwood before applying the varnish.

        2

_____

_____

_____

_____

(d) The handle was made from a blank using a centre lathe similar to the one shown in the photo below.

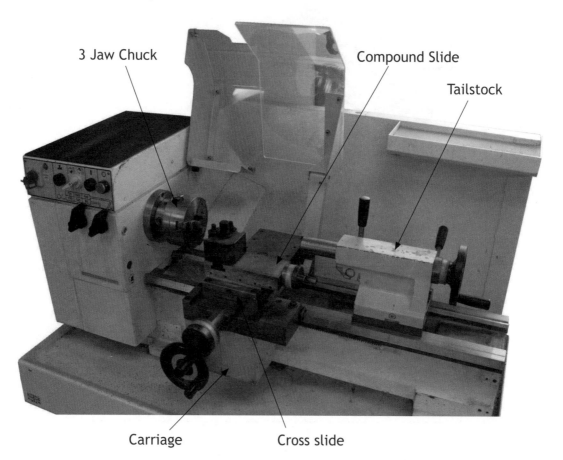

3 Jaw Chuck   Compound Slide

Tailstock

Carriage   Cross slide

The handle consists of two parts as shown in the diagram below:

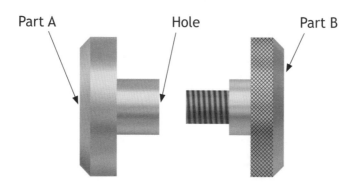

Part A   Hole   Part B

MARKS | DO NOT WRITE IN THIS MARGIN

1. **(d)** **(continued)**

Part B has been knurled.

(i) Describe the process of knurling on a centre lathe.

3

_____

_____

_____

_____

(ii) State the functional reason for knurling Part B.

1

_____

_____

_____

_____

Part A was created from a blank roughly sawn from a piece of aluminium bar as shown in the diagram below.

Original blank   Overall form of Part A

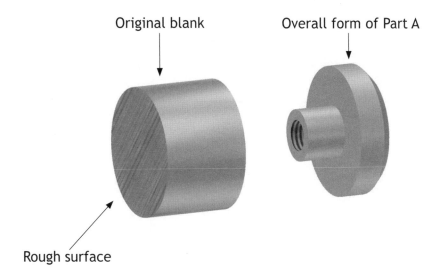

Rough surface

(iii) State **two** processes that would be carried out on a centre lathe to manufacture the overall form of Part A from a blank.

2

_____

_____

_____

_____

MARKS | DO NOT WRITE IN THIS MARGIN

1. **(continued)**

The drawer of the TV stand contains a thermoplastic facing. The photos below show the piece of plastic cut to size and the rough edge of the plastic after sawing.

Plastic cut to size   Rough

(e) Describe **four** stages required to create a smooth surface finish on the sawn edges of the piece of plastic.   **4**

_____

_____

_____

_____

Total marks 24

SECTION 2 — 36 marks

Attempt ALL questions

2.

The market for hairdryers has increased over recent years and designers have to consider various factors in their designs.

(a) Describe in what ways the design of hairdryers, as shown in the photo above, could have been influenced by ergonomics.

6

_____

_____

_____

_____

_____

_____

_____

_____

_____

_____

_____

_____

_____

_____

MARKS | DO NOT WRITE IN THIS MARGIN

2. (continued)

(b) Before producing a design specification for a hairdryer, the designer would have researched various design factors.

Explain why the following design factors would be researched when designing hairdryers.

(i) Aesthetics

1

_____

_____

_____

_____

(ii) Performance

1

_____

_____

_____

_____

(iii) Materials

1

_____

_____

_____

_____

Total marks   9

3.

Over recent years, there has been a steady increase in the number of electronic products available to consumers in the marketplace.

(a) Explain the term **"Technology Push"** with reference to **electronic products**.

2

_____

_____

_____

_____

_____

_____

All of the electronic products shown in the photo above were launched under a successful brand name.

(b) Describe **two** benefits to the designer of launching a product under a successful brand name.

2

_____

_____

_____

_____

_____

Total marks   4

4. Designers often make models of their designs as they work through the design process as shown in the photos below.

Model of an iron

Model of a vacuum head

(a) Describe **two** benefits a designer could gain from modelling.

2

_____

_____

_____

_____

_____

_____

(b) State the names of **two** modelling materials and explain why **each** would be suitable for building models.

2

_____

_____

_____

_____

_____

_____

MARKS | DO NOT WRITE IN THIS MARGIN

4. **(continued)**

In addition to physical modelling, designers often use computer generated models as shown in the photos below.

Physical foam and card model

Computer generated model

(c) State **two** advantages to the designer of using a computer generated model rather than a physical model.

2

_____

_____

_____

_____

_____

Rapid prototyping is another type of model used by designers as shown in the photo below.

Rapid prototype of a mobile phone casing

(d) Describe **one** benefit that rapid prototyping offers the designer.

1

_____

_____

_____

Total marks   7

5. A typical classroom chair is shown in the photo below.

Seat

Tubular steel frame

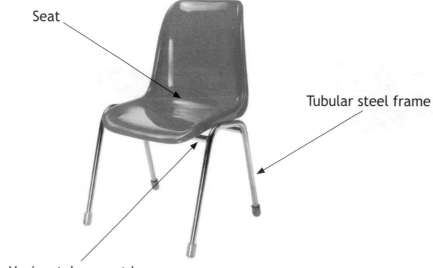

Horizontal support bar

(a) (i) State the name of a suitable material for the seat of the chair. **1**

_____

(ii) Give **two** reasons why the material you have stated would be suitable for use in this type of product. **2**

_____

_____

_____

_____

_____

_____

(iii) State a suitable manufacturing process that could be used to manufacture the seat of the chair. **1**

_____

MARKS | DO NOT WRITE IN THIS MARGIN

5.   (continued)

Tubular steel was used to manufacture the frame of the chair.

(b)   (i)   State a joining technique that could be used to permanently join the horizontal support bars to the rest of the frame.

1

(ii)   State the name of a suitable finish for the tubular steel frame.

1

(c)   Standard components, as shown in the photos above, are used in many products and are used to join the seat to the frame of the school chair. Explain **two** advantages to the manufacturer of using "standard components".

2

Total marks   8

6. Two different types of coffee machines are shown below.

Coffee shop coffee machine   Home coffee machine

The home coffee machine allows consumers to produce coffee shop style drinks in their own home.

In order to ensure the product would be a success, the designers would have had to carry out a detailed evaluation of the prototype.

(a) Describe **one** evaluation technique that may have been used when evaluating **each** of the following design factors.

(*Note: a different technique should be used for each factor.*)

(i) Ease of use   2

_____

_____

_____

_____

_____

(ii) Aesthetics   2

_____

_____

_____

_____

_____

MARKS

6. (a) (continued)

    (iii) Value for money   **2**

_____

_____

_____

_____

_____

(b) Describe the roles of **two** design team members who would have been involved in the evaluation of the home coffee machine prototype.   **2**

_____

_____

_____

_____

_____

Total marks   8

[END OF SPECIMEN QUESTION PAPER]

Model Paper 1

Whilst this Model Practice Paper has been specially commissioned by Hodder Gibson for use as practice for the National 5 exams, the key reference documents remain the SQA Specimen Paper 2013 and the SQA Past Paper 2014.

N5

National
Qualifications
MODEL PAPER 1

Design and Manufacture

Duration — 1 hour and 30 minutes

Total marks — 60

SECTION 1 — 24 marks

Attempt ALL questions.

SECTION 2 — 36 marks

Attempt ALL questions.

Read every question carefully before you attempt it.

Write your answers clearly in the spaces provided, using **blue** or **black** ink.

Show all working and units where appropriate.

Before leaving the examination room you must give this booklet to the Invigilator.
If you do not, you may lose all the marks for this paper.

HODDER
GIBSON
LEARN MORE

SECTION 1 — 24 marks

Attempt ALL questions

1. A small storage container is shown below.

(a) The container was manufactured mainly from softwood.

State the name of **two** suitable softwoods that could have been used.   **2**

_____

_____

(b) The back of the container is made from plywood as shown below.

1. (b) (continued) MARKS DO NOT WRITE IN THIS MARGIN

(i) Describe the benefits of using plywood for the back of the container. 2

(ii) State the name of **two** other manufactured boards that could have been used. 2

(c) The drawer of the container is shown below.

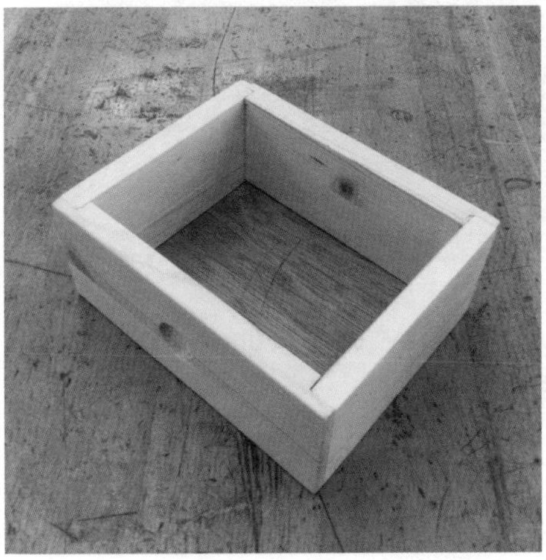

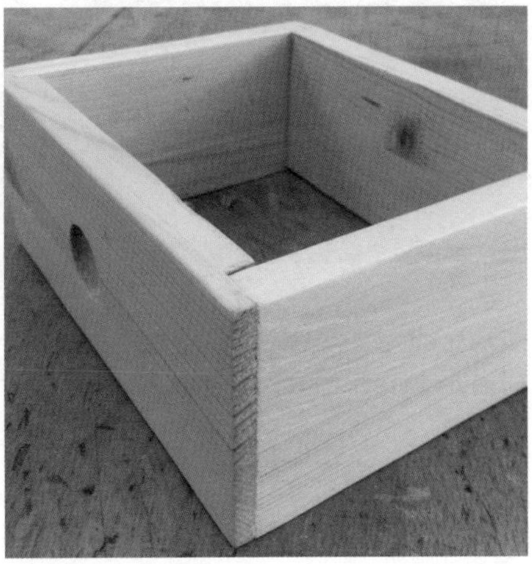

(i) State the name of **two** suitable joining techniques that could have been used at each corner of the drawer. 2

(ii) Describe, with reference to tools, the way that one of the joints you have named above could be manufactured in the workshop using hand tools. 3

The drawer has a 20mm diameter hole for opening instead of a handle.

(iii) Describe, with reference to tools and machinery, the way that the 20mm hole could have been manufactured in the workshop. 3

1. (continued) **MARKS** DO NOT WRITE IN THIS MARGIN

The container has been finished with wax.

(d) Describe the benefits of using wax to finish the surfaces of the container. **2**

____

____

(e) The decorative plastic photo-frame shown below was added to the top of the container.

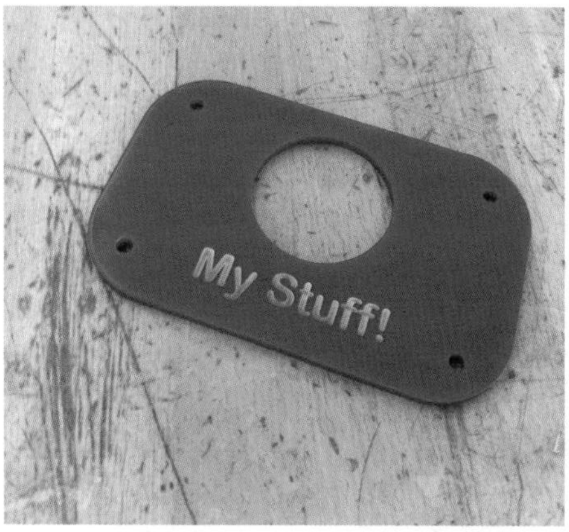

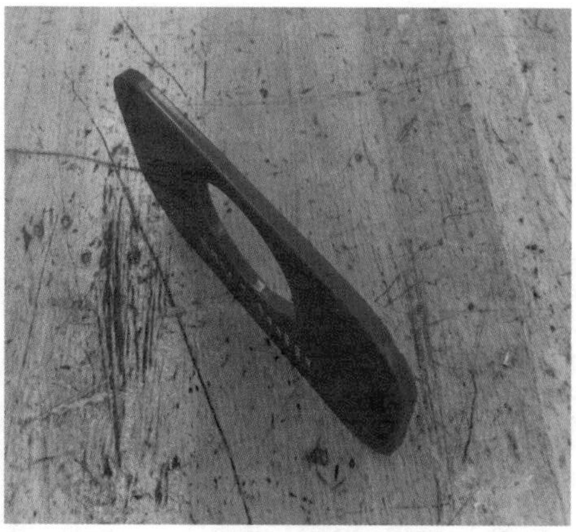

(i) Describe, with reference to tools, the way the four holes would have been marked out in the workshop. **3**

____

____

____

(ii) Describe the stages that would be carried out to make the edges of the plastic smooth and shiny. **4**

____

____

____

____

The screws and eyelets used to join the plastic to the container were manufactured from a non-ferrous metal

(iii) State the name of a suitable non-ferrous metal. **1**

____

Total marks 24

SECTION 2 — 36 marks

Attempt ALL questions

2. Computer mice are shown below.

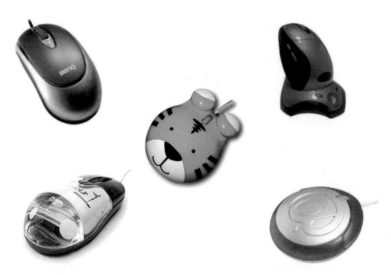

Before producing a specification for a computer mouse the designer would have researched various design issues.

With reference to a computer mouse, state **four** design issues which would have been researched and explain why each of these design issues is important.

5

_____

_____

_____

_____

_____

_____

_____

_____

_____

_____

_____

_____

_____

3. A child's activity toy is shown below.

Describe how the design of the activity toy has been influenced by ergonomics.   **6**

_____

_____

_____

_____

_____

_____

_____

_____

_____

_____

_____

_____

_____

_____

_____

_____

_____

_____

4. During the design process, a designer will use various materials to build models.

(a) State **two** reasons why the designer would build models.   **2**

_____

_____

4. (continued)

MARKS | DO NOT WRITE IN THIS MARGIN

(b) State the name of **two** materials that could be used to produce models and explain why each material is suitable. 4

(Note: a different explanation should be given for each material.)

____

____

____

____

Total marks 6

5. A portable gas camping stove is shown below.

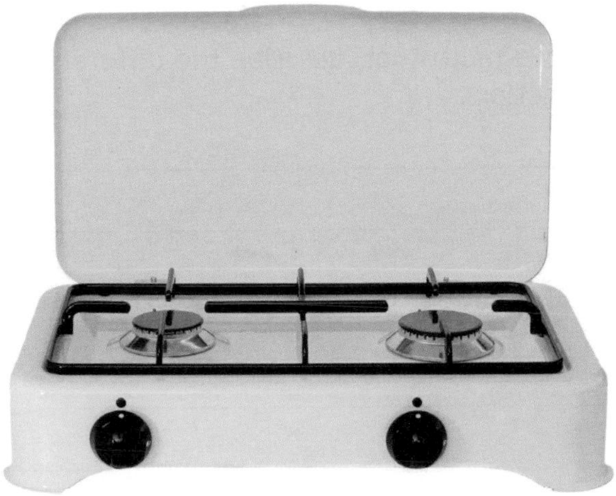

(a) Describe how each of the following issues has influenced the design of the camping stove.

(i) Environment 2

____

____

(ii) Safety 2

____

____

(b) The camping stove could be described as being attractive to a niche market. Explain the term "**niche market**". 2

____

____

____

Total marks 6

6. A pocket multi-tool manufactured from stainless steel is shown below.

(a) With reference to the above multi-tool, describe the difference between primary and secondary functions.

2

(b) Describe a technique that could be used to evaluate the ease of use of the multi-tool.

2

(c) Describe the aesthetic qualities of the multi-tool.

2

(d) State **one** reason why the designer has chosen stainless steel for this product.

1

(e) State **two** methods of applying a coloured finish to the handles.

2

Total marks   **9**

MARKS

7. The ability to generate ideas is an important aspect of a designer's work.

(a) State **two** idea generation techniques.

2

_____

_____

(b) Describe how one of these techniques would be carried out.

2

_____

_____

_____

_____

Total marks 4

[END OF MODEL PRACTICE PAPER]

Model Paper 2

Whilst this Model Practice Paper has been specially commissioned by Hodder Gibson for use as practice for the National 5 exams, the key reference documents remain the SQA Specimen Paper 2013 and the SQA Past Paper 2014.

National Qualifications
MODEL PAPER 2

Design and Manufacture

Duration — 1 hour and 30 minutes

Total marks — 60

SECTION 1 — 24 marks

Attempt ALL questions.

SECTION 2 — 36 marks

Attempt ALL questions.

Read every question carefully before you attempt it.

Write your answers clearly in the spaces provided, using **blue** or **black** ink.

Show all working and units where appropriate.

Before leaving the examination room you must give this booklet to the Invigilator.
If you do not, you may lose all the marks for this paper.

SECTION 1 – 24 marks

Attempt ALL questions

1. A bird box is shown below.

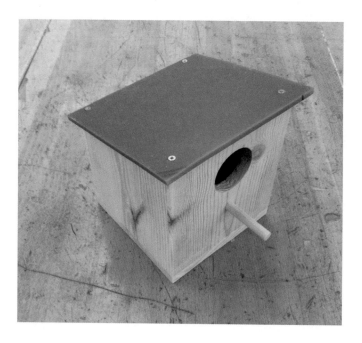

(a) The bird box was manufactured mainly from softwood.

(i) State the name of a suitable softwood that could have been used in the manufacture of the bird box.

_____   **1**

(ii) Describe the environmental benefits of choosing softwood rather than hardwood.   **2**

_____

_____

(b) A peg has been fitted to the bird box as shown above.

(i) Describe, with reference to tools, the way the position of the peg would have been marked out in the workshop.   **3**

_____

_____

_____

(ii) Describe a permanent method of joining the peg to the bird box.   **3**

_____

_____

_____

1. (continued)

(c) The corner of the bird box is shown below.

(i) State the name of **two** suitable joining techniques that could have been used at the corners of the bird box.

2

_____

_____

(ii) Describe the way that one of the joints you have named above could be manufactured in the workshop using hand tools.

3

_____

_____

_____

The bird box has a 35mm diameter opening to allow birds to enter.

(iii) Describe, with reference to tools and equipment, the way that the 35mm hole could have been manufactured in the workshop.

3

_____

_____

_____

_____

The bird box has been finished with clear varnish.

(d) Describe the benefits of using clear varnish to finish the surfaces of the bird box.

2

_____

_____

1. (continued)

(e) The roof of the bird box has been manufactured from plastic as shown below.

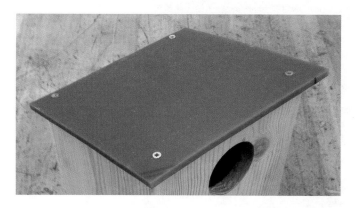

Describe the properties of thermoplastic that make it suitable for the roof of the bird box.

3

_____

_____

_____

_____

(f) Screws were used to join the plastic roof to the main body of the bird box.

Describe an alternative method of joining the roof to the main body that would allow the bird box to be easily accessed for cleaning.

2

_____

_____

_____

_____

Total marks 24

SECTION 2 – 36 marks

Attempt ALL questions

MARKS | DO NOT WRITE IN THIS MARGIN

2. IPod docking stations are shown below.

Before producing a specification for an IPod docking station the designer would have researched various issues.

With reference to IPod docking stations:

State **four** design issues which would have been researched and explain why each of these design issues is important.   **5**

_____

_____

_____

_____

_____

_____

_____

_____

_____

_____

_____

3. Designers use a variety of different graphic techniques in order to communicate.

State **two** graphic techniques, which the designer could use to effectively communicate with:

(a) The client   **2**

_____

(b) The manufacturer   **2**

_____

(c) Other designers   **2**

_____

Total marks   **6**

4. A toaster is shown below.

The manufacturer wishes to carry out an evaluation of the toaster.

Describe an evaluation activity that could be carried out for each of the following aspects of the toaster.

(Note: a different technique must be used for each aspect.)

(a) Ease of use

2

_____

_____

(b) Aesthetics

2

_____

_____

(c) Value for money

2

_____

_____

(d) The speed of toasting

2

_____

_____

Total marks   8

5. Children's cutlery is shown below.

MARKS

Explain why the designer would consider **each** of following areas during the designing of children's cutlery.

(a) Ergonomics

1

_____

(b) Safety

1

_____

(c) Aesthetics

1

_____

(d) Materials

1

_____

Total marks **4**

6. The computer desk shown below was supplied as a flat-pack.

MARKS

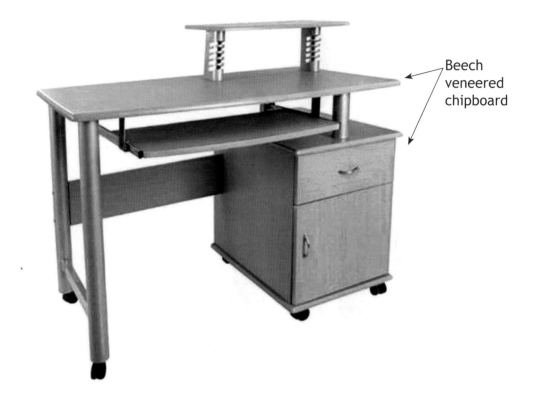

Beech veneered chipboard

(a) State **two advantages** to the **consumer** of flat-packed furniture.   2

_____

_____

(b) State **two** advantages of using beech veneered chipboard for the computer desk rather than using solid beech.   2

_____

_____

(c) Knock down fittings are often used in the construction of flat-packed furniture.

Explain the term **"knock down fittings"**.   1

_____

(d) Flat-packed furniture can be aimed at a particular market niche.

Explain the term **"market niche"** with reference to flat packed furniture.   2

_____

_____

Total marks   7

7. A cordless vacuum cleaner is shown below.

Trigger

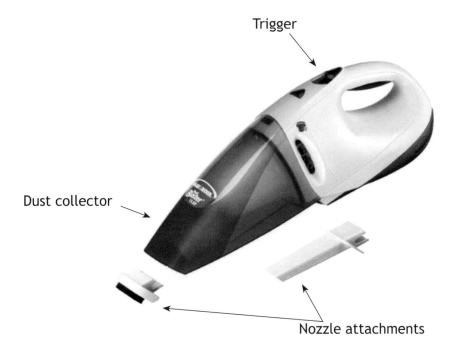

Dust collector

Nozzle attachments

Describe how the design of the cordless vacuum cleaner has been influenced by ergonomics.

6

_____

_____

_____

_____

_____

_____

_____

_____

_____

_____

_____

_____

_____

_____

_____

_____

_____

_____

_____

[END OF MODEL PRACTICE PAPER]

Model Paper 3

Whilst this Model Practice Paper has been specially commissioned by Hodder Gibson for use as practice for the National 5 exams, the key reference documents remain the SQA Specimen Paper 2013 and the SQA Past Paper 2014.

National Qualifications
MODEL PAPER 3

Design and Manufacture

Duration — 1 hour and 30 minutes

Total marks — 60

SECTION 1 — 24 marks

Attempt ALL questions.

SECTION 2 — 36 marks

Attempt ALL questions.

Read every question carefully before you attempt it.

Write your answers clearly in the spaces provided, using **blue** or **black** ink.

Show all working and units where appropriate.

Before leaving the examination room you must give this booklet to the Invigilator.
If you do not, you may lose all the marks for this paper.

SECTION 1 – 24 marks

Attempt ALL questions

1. A small display unit is shown below.

(a) The unit was manufactured mainly from pine.

    (i) State the name of one other softwood that could have been used in the manufacture of the unit.

        1

_____

    (ii) Explain the reasons why designers often choose softwood rather than hardwood to manufacture products like the unit.

        2

_____

_____

(b) The main parts of the unit have been joined together using cross-halving joints.

1. (b) (continued) **MARKS** DO NOT WRITE IN THIS MARGIN

Describe, with reference to tools, the processes that would have been carried out in the workshop to manufacture the cross-halving joint. **3**

(c) The support used at the back of the unit is shown below.

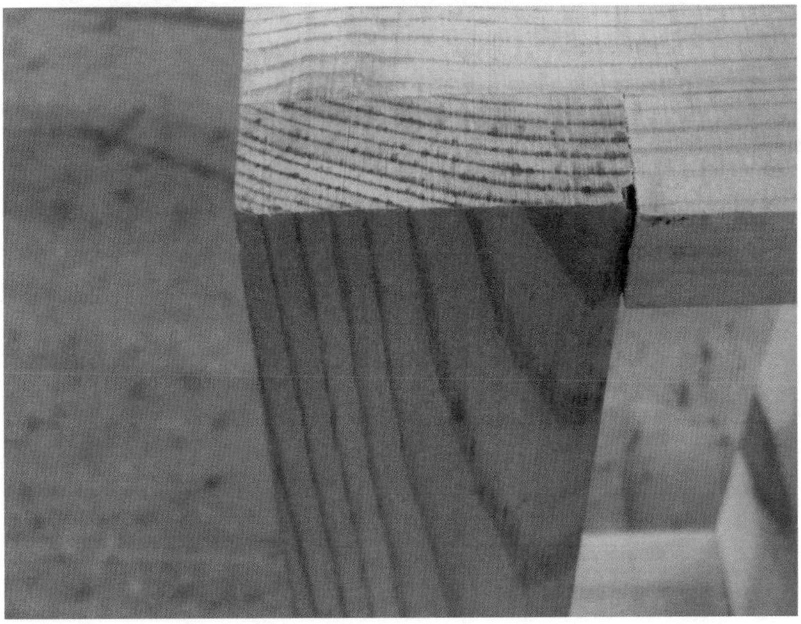

A simple lap joint was used to join the two parts together.

Describe, with reference to tools, the way the lap joint could have been marked out in the workshop. **3**

1. (continued)

(d) The unit has two 6mm diameter metal uprights to support the front of the shelves.

 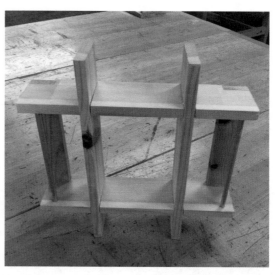

(i) State the name of **two** suitable non-ferrous metals that could have been used.

2

_____

_____

(ii) The metal has been cut from a long section of bar to 130mm long.

Describe, with reference to tools, the processes that could have been used to mark out and cut the bar to length in the workshop.

3

_____

_____

_____

_____

_____

_____

(iii) After the bars have been cut, the ends could be sharp and unsafe.

Describe, with reference to tools the processes that could be used to smooth the ends of the bars to make them safe.

3

_____

_____

_____

_____

_____

_____

1. (d) (continued)   MARKS

    (iv) Describe a method of permanently joining the metal bars to the wooden shelves.   2

_____

_____

_____

_____

_____

_____

(e) Before applying wax as a finish to the wood, the surfaces would need to be prepared.

Describe the processes that could be carried out to ensure the surfaces were ready to be waxed.   3

_____

_____

_____

_____

_____

_____

(f) Describe the benefits of using wax to finish the wooden surfaces of the unit.   2

_____

_____

_____

_____

_____

_____

Total marks 24

SECTION 2 — 36 marks

Attempt ALL questions

2. Salt and pepper sets are shown below.

Before producing a specification for a salt and pepper set the designer would have researched various issues.

State **four** design issues which would have been researched and explain why each of these design issues is important.

5

_____

_____

_____

_____

_____

_____

_____

_____

_____

_____

_____

3. A pair of training shoes is shown below.

(a) Describe how consumer demand influences the design of training shoes.   **2**

_____

_____

_____

_____

_____

(b) Advertising is one technique used to increase sales of training shoes.

Describe **two** other techniques which could also be used to increase sales.   **4**

_____

_____

_____

_____

_____

Total marks   6

4. A CAD model of a proposed printer design is shown below.

The manufacturer wishes to carry out market research activities about the printer.

(a) Describe an activity that could be carried out for each of the following aspects of the proposed printer.

(Note: a different activity must be used for each aspect.)

   (i) Value for money

2

   (ii) Aesthetics

2

MARKS | DO NOT WRITE IN THIS MARGIN

4. (continued)

(b) Describe the advantages to the manufacturer of using CAD modelling during the design of the printer.   3

_____

_____

_____

(c) State **three** techniques (**other than CAD modelling**) which the designer could use to effectively communicate with other members of the design team.   3

_____

_____

_____

Total marks 10

5. The ability to generate ideas is an important aspect of a designer's work.

(a) State **two** idea generation techniques.   2

_____

_____

(b) Describe how one of the techniques you have named above would be carried out by the designer.   2

_____

_____

_____

_____

_____

_____

Total marks   4

MARKS | DO NOT WRITE IN THIS MARGIN

6. Five products are shown below with a list of manufacturing processes.

Match each product or part of product with the most suitable manufacturing process from the list.

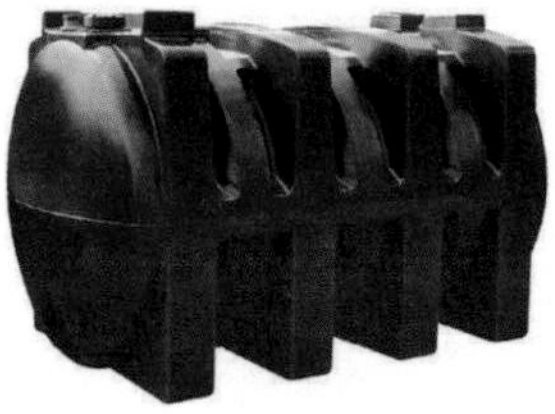

A Oil tank

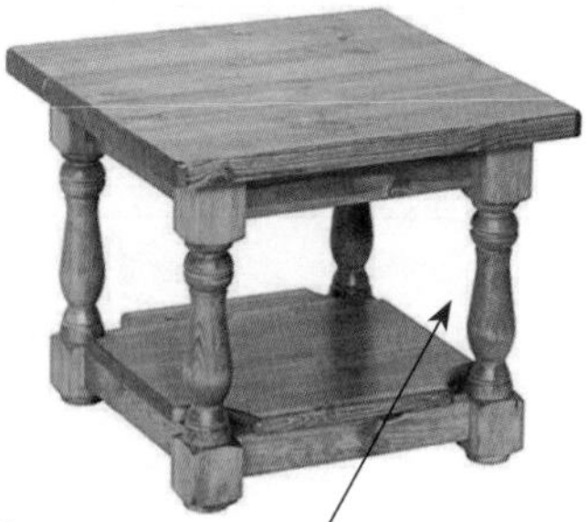

B Table leg

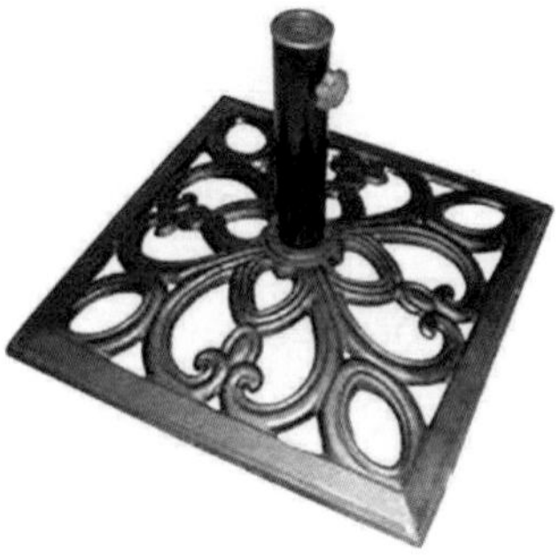

C Metal parasol stand

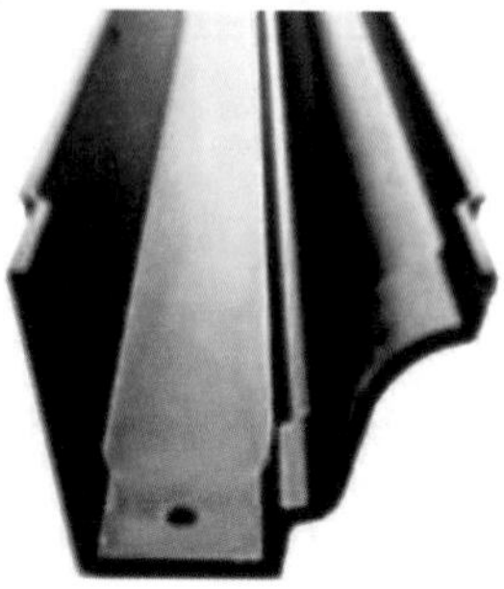

D Houehold guttering

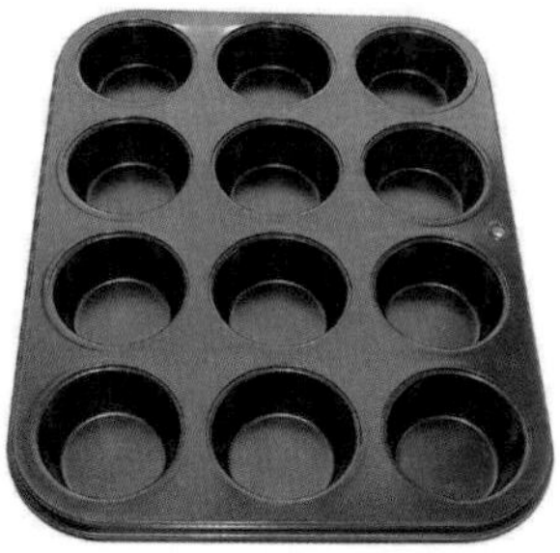

E Metal muffin tray

- **Manufacturing Processes**
- Soldering
- Rotational Moulding
- Press-forming
- Extrusion
- Compression moulding
- Injection moulding
- Sand casting
- Laminating
- Turning

(a) __________ 1

(b) __________ 1

(c) __________ 1

(d) __________ 1

(e) __________ 1

Total marks 5

7. A hand-held game is shown below.

Describe how the design of the hand-held game has been influenced by ergonomics.

_____

_____

_____

_____

_____

_____

_____

_____

_____

_____

_____

_____

_____

Total marks   **6**

[END OF MODEL PRACTICE PAPER]

NATIONAL 5

2014

N5

National
Qualifications
2014

Mark

X719/75/01

Design and Manufacture

TUESDAY, 27 MAY
1:00 PM – 2:30 PM

Fill in these boxes and read what is printed below.

Full name of centre

Town

Forename(s)

Surname

Number of seat

Date of birth

Day	Month	Year
D D	M M	Y Y

Scottish candidate number

Total marks — 60

SECTION 1 — 24 marks

Attempt ALL questions.

SECTION 2 — 36 marks

Attempt ALL questions.

Write your answers clearly in the spaces provided in this booklet. Additional space for answers is provided at the end of this booklet. If you use this space you must clearly identify the question number you are attempting.

Use **blue** or **black** ink.

Before leaving the examination room you must give this booklet to the Invigilator; if you do not, you may lose all the marks for this paper.

MARKS | DO NOT WRITE IN THIS MARGIN

SECTION 1 — 24 marks

Attempt ALL questions

1. A chess box is shown below.

Chess board

Aluminium handle

Corner joint

(a) Hardwood was used for some of the squares of the chess board.

   (i) State the name of a hardwood that could have been used for the squares.

     1

_____

   (ii) Describe **two** benefits of using hardwoods for the manufacture of this product.

     2

_____

_____

(b) A comb joint has been used at each corner.

State the name of **two** alternative joints that could have been used at each corner.

     2

_____

_____

(c) Clear varnish was used as a surface finish for the chess box.

   (i) Describe **two** benefits of using clear varnish as a surface finish for the chess box.

     2

_____

_____

MARKS | DO NOT WRITE IN THIS MARGIN

1. (c) (continued)

(ii) Describe **two** stages in the preparation of the wood before applying the varnish.

2

_____

_____

The plastic tray shown below was vacuum formed and is used to hold the chess pieces. The wooden pattern used in the process is also shown.

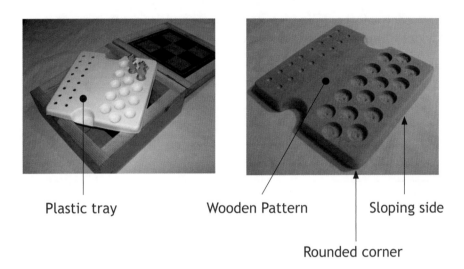

Plastic tray   Wooden Pattern   Sloping side

Rounded corner

(d) Explain the reason for the following features in the wooden pattern.

(i) Rounded corners _____ 1

_____

(ii) Sloping sides _____ 1

_____

(iii) A thermoplastic was used for the tray.

Describe **two** benefits of using a thermoplastic for this type of product.

2

_____

_____

_____

_____

[Turn over

MARKS | DO NOT WRITE IN THIS MARGIN

1. (continued)

(e) The aluminium handle shown below was manufactured using a centre lathe.

Chamfer ——⦁   ⦁—— Parallel Turned Dowel

Describe how **each** of the following processes would be carried out on the centre lathe to manufacture the handle.

(i) Chamfering   2

_____

_____

_____

_____

(ii) Parallel turning   2

_____

_____

_____

_____

(iii) A change of speed may be required when using a centre lathe.

State **two** reasons why a change in lathe speed may be necessary.   2

_____

_____

_____

_____

_____

MARKS

1. (continued)

(f) The aluminium chess pieces shown below were commercially produced by the process of die casting.

(i) State **two** reasons for using aluminium for the chess pieces.   2

_____

_____

_____

_____

(ii) State **three** benefits of using die casting to manufacture the chess pieces.   3

_____

_____

_____

_____

_____

_____

Total marks 24

[Turn over

MARKS | DO NOT WRITE IN THIS MARGIN

SECTION 2 — 36 marks

Attempt ALL questions

2. The 2012 Olympic success of Team GB caused an increased interest in all forms of cycling for all ages.

(a) Describe how ergonomics has influenced the design of bicycles.   6

MARKS | DO NOT WRITE IN THIS MARGIN

2. (continued)

(b) Before producing a design specification for a bicycle, the designer would have researched various design factors.

Explain why the following design factors would be researched when designing bicycles.

(i) Durability   1

_____

_____

_____

_____

(ii) Ease of maintenance   1

_____

_____

_____

_____

(iii) Aesthetics   1

_____

_____

_____

_____

Total marks   9

[Turn over

3. The environmental impact of a product can often influence our buying decisions.

Explain ways in which designers could reduce the environmental impact of their products.

(*You may wish to refer to products with which you are familiar.*)   3

_____

_____

_____

_____

_____

_____

_____

_____

_____

_____

_____

MARKS | DO NOT WRITE IN THIS MARGIN

4. Designers use a range of graphic techniques to communicate their designs.

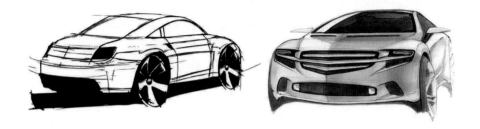

(a) State the name of **one** graphic technique that the designer may use at each of the following stages of the design process **and** explain why it would be suitable.

(*A different graphic technique must be used for each stage.*)

(i) Initial ideas   2

_____

_____

_____

_____

(ii) Planning for manufacture   2

_____

_____

_____

_____

[Turn over

MARKS | DO NOT WRITE IN THIS MARGIN

4. (continued)

(b) Designers often use models as well as a range of graphic techniques.

State the name of **two** modelling materials and explain why each would be suitable for building models.

(*A different explanation must be given for each material.*)   4

_____

_____

_____

_____

_____

_____

_____

_____

Total marks   8

MARKS | DO NOT WRITE IN THIS MARGIN

5. A stainless steel colander is shown below.

(a) (i) Give **two** reasons why stainless steel would be suitable for the colander.

2

_____

_____

_____

_____

(ii) The colander was mass produced.

Describe **two** benefits to the manufacturer of mass production techniques.

2

_____

_____

_____

_____

[Turn over

MARKS | DO NOT WRITE IN THIS MARGIN

5. (continued)

(b) Colanders can also be manufactured from plastic as shown below.

State the name of a suitable process for manufacturing colanders from plastic.

1

_____

(c) Manufacturers are increasingly using CNC and CADCAM technologies to make their products.

Describe the impact that these technologies have on the manufacturer.

3

_____

_____

_____

_____

_____

_____

_____

_____

_____

_____

_____

Total marks   8

MARKS | DO NOT WRITE IN THIS MARGIN

6. An electric razor is shown below.

The manufacturer wishes to carry out an evaluation of the razor.

(a) Describe a suitable user trial to evaluate the ergonomics of the razor.   2

_____

_____

_____

_____

(b) State **two** key questions that would be included in a survey to evaluate the aesthetics of the razor.   2

_____

_____

_____

_____

[Turn over for Question 6 (c) on *Page fourteen*

MARKS | DO NOT WRITE IN THIS MARGIN

6. (continued)

(c) There are a wide variety of razors available on the market today.

With such a large selection, designers need to find ways of marketing their product in order to make it stand out from the competition.

Describe **two** marketing techniques that a design team may use to promote their product.

2

_____

_____

_____

_____

_____

_____

(d) Designers often have to generate new ideas to stay ahead of their competitors.

Describe **one** idea generation technique that they could use.

2

_____

_____

_____

_____

_____

_____

Total marks   8

[END OF QUESTION PAPER]

ADDITIONAL SPACE FOR ANSWERS

ADDITIONAL SPACE FOR ANSWERS

SQA AND HODDER GIBSON NATIONAL 5 DESIGN AND MANUFACTURE 2014

SECTION 1

1. (a) (i) *Any one of the following:*
- Hardboard
- Plywood
- MDF

(ii) *A description that covers three of the following benefits:*
- Low cost
- Strong (enough)
- Uses recycled materials
- Available in large boards
- Can be cut to any shape
- Easy to machine
- Uniform thickness
- Durable
- Readily available
- Any other suitable response

(iii) *A description that covers two of the following issues:*
- Softwood trees grow faster
- Softwoods grow in farmed forests
- Using hardwoods endangers rainforests

(b) (i) It supports the shelf across its width.

(ii) *A description that covers the following three stages:*
- Marking out two parallel lines and required depth
- Cutting slot between the two parallel lines
- Levelling the slot to a consistent depth

(c) (i) *A description that covers two of the following benefits:*
- Enhances appearance of softwood
- Allows you to see the natural wood (unlike paint)
- Hard surface protects against bumps/scratches
- Hard surface protects against bumps/scratches
- Prevents softwood drying out and splitting/warping

(ii) *A description that includes two of the following stages:*
- Remove pencil marks/blemishes with sandpaper
- Wet wood to raise the grain
- Sand lightly

(d) (i) *A description that includes the following three points:*
- Fit the knurling tool
- Slow the speed of the lathe down
- Slowly move the cross-slide towards Part B until it makes the knurled pattern to the required depth

(ii) It provides grip for the user.

(iii) *Any two of the following processes:*
- Face off the ends
- Chamfer the edge
- Parallel turn the smaller diameter

(e) *A description that includes four of the following stages:*
- Through filing
- Draw filing
- Wet/dry paper
- Emery cloth
- Steel wool
- Polish

SECTION 2

2. (a) **Anthropometrics:**

The length of the handle will have taken into consideration the male 95th percentile dimension for hand width. This would ensure that as many people as possible could grip the handle comfortably.

The designer would have to find the index finger width/circumference to determine the size of any switches or buttons to ensure as many people as possible could use the hairdryer with ease. If buttons are too small, people could find them difficult to locate and press.

Physiology:

The strength or power required to press the on/off button would have been considered to ensure users do not have to apply too much force. This excess force could result in the product being hard to use or even worse, causing injury.

The strength or power required to operate the hinge of the green hairdryer would have to be considered by the designer. It needs to be easy to fold but not so loose as to fold during operation.

The material used for the handles would have been considered to ensure the user can grip them comfortably. The user's hands could be damp from their wet hair so it is important that a slippery material is not selected.

Psychology:

A colour which contrasts with the main body of the hairdryer could be chosen to make the buttons stand out. This will make it obvious to the user which parts need to be pressed or adjusted to operate the hairdryer.

A style or pattern on the hairdryer makes it appeal to a user's sense of style.

(b) (i) Aesthetics would have to be considered when designing a hairdryer as it would have to appeal to the target market, whilst standing out against the competition.

(ii) Performance would have to be considered when designing a hairdryer to ensure it safely dried hair in a reasonable amount of time.

(iii) Materials would have to be considered when designing a hairdryer to make sure it did not heat up when in use and burn the user.

3. (a) *An explanation that includes two of the following points.*
Products would be redesigned where:
- Changes in manufacturing technology become available allowing electronic products to be manufactured at a lesser cost, more quickly or easily
- Changes in materials technology become available allowing more complex or interesting shapes and forms to be manufactured, e.g. allowing them to be lighter, smaller, miniaturised, or more attractive to market
- Changes in technology become available allowing electronic products to perform additional functions, e.g. motion sensors or GPS

(b) Benefits of launching a product under a successful brand name are that it is:
- Less risky for the designer
- The brand will be recognised by consumers
- People will be more willing to spend their money on the product if they have used the brand before
- Successful brands have more money available for advertising

4. (a) • Models will allow the designer to test/check the proportion and ergonomics of the product by allowing them to touch, hold and interact with it. They could then make changes as they develop the design further.
- Models could be used to communicate the designs with other members of the design team. It may be easier for others to understand the design or parts of it in a 3D model rather than a sketch.

(b) Materials such as paper, card, MDF, wire, expanded foam, clay, balsa wood, sheet plastic could be listed. *Reasons for suitability may include:*
- Low cost
- Easy to work with and shape
- Quick to work with
- Give good results
- Any other suitable answer

(c) Possible advantages:
- Time
- Quality
- Ease of communication between designers and offices, e.g. email
- Ability to rapid prototype
- Ability to add material surface effects
- Can be used for marketing
- Any other suitable answer

(d) Possible benefits:
- Quick to produce
- Can be tested
- Communication with design team and clients
- Material finishes can be applied to make it look realistic
- Can be used for marketing
- Any other relevant answer

5. (a) (i) *Any one of the following:*
- Polypropylene
- ABS

(ii) Reasons could include:
- Strength and durability relating to repeated daily use
- Strength to weight ratio relating to portability around school/class
- Aesthetics — inbuilt colour, making it more attractive to the user
- Cost — school budgets
- Suitable for manufacturing process
- Any other suitable answer

(iii) Injection moulding

(b) (i) Welding

(ii) Suitable finishes:
- Paint
- Spray paint
- Plastic dip coating

(c) *An explanation that includes any two of the following points:*
- Cheaper than producing them yourself
- Reliable
- Variety available for different jobs
- Secure fixing
- Semi-permanent fixings
- Any other suitable answer

6. (a) (i) Ease of use:
A user trial could be used to evaluate the ease of use of the coffee machine. The designer may have asked consumers to make a cup of coffee whilst watching them to see if they had any problems in doing so. For example, finding switches, removing lids, etc. Any problems noted could then be adjusted or changed before manufacturing the product.

(ii) Aesthetics:
- A survey or questionnaire could be used to evaluate the aesthetics of the coffee machine.
- Consumers could be shown a prototype of the product and asked their opinions on shape, form, colour, etc to ensure the designer has made it appealing to the target market.

(iii) Value for money:
A product comparison could have been used to evaluate if the coffee machine is good value for money. Similar products could be researched to find out how much they sell for, as well as the functions they offer. This would help give the team an idea of whether people would be willing to pay for their design or not.

(b) *A description that includes any two of the following:*
- Market researcher/marketing team — would have been involved in evaluating how well the coffee maker met the needs and wants of the market or how competitively priced it is
- Designer — would evaluate how well the design met the overall requirements of the design brief
- Ergonomist — would have evaluated how easy the product was to use in terms of human factors, e.g. comfort, etc
- Accountant — would have evaluated how financially viable the product would be, how much it has cost to design and produce
- Retailer — would have evaluated how successful the product was in terms of sales

NATIONAL 5 DESIGN & MANUFACTURE MODEL PAPER 1

SECTION 1

1. (a) Pine, Spruce

(b) (i) Plywood is strong in all directions and will not warp or bend after fitting.

(ii) MDF, hardboard

(c) (i) Lap joint, dovetail joint

(ii) **Lap joint:** after marking out the joint with a try square, marking gauge and rule, you would cut down halfway through the wood with a tenon saw. Then you would chisel out the waste wood with a bevel edged chisel. Finally you could use a hand router to smooth the bottom of the lap joint.

(iii) **20mm hole:** after marking out with a rule and a try square, you would fit a forstener bit to the pillar drill. You would then drill slowly through the wood to make sure you don't split it at the back.

(d) Wax makes the container look good and it also makes it more durable and helps to protect the wood from rotting.

(e) (i) The four holes would have been marked out by using a rule, scriber and engineers square: the rule would be used to measure along the edge of the acrylic to the desired size, this would be marked by the scriber. Then the engineers square would be used with the scriber to mark out the positions of the holes.

(ii) There are four usual stages, these are cross file, draw file, wet and dry paper or block and finally applying polish with a cloth.

(iii) Brass

SECTION 2

2. The designer would research: Function, ergonomics, durability and safety.

- **Function:** The mouse will need to perform several operations such as scrolling and multi-button use.
- **Ergonomics:** The mouse will need to be the right size for most users' hands.
- **Durability:** The mouse will need to be able to withstand being used every day and not wear away.
- **Safety:** The mouse has some electrical connection and therefore it will need to be safe for the user to hold it and not get an electric shock.

One mark for the four issues, one mark for each explanation.

3. *Candidates have three possible routes to go down in their response: anthropometrics, physiology and psychology. There is no requirement to refer to any of these areas by name. Typical responses within each aspect are shown below. Six suitable responses will gain six marks. Any suitable answer relating human dimensions and relevant aspect of the activity toy should be awarded one mark, e.g. The slide width has been designed to suit child hip breadth.*

Other suitable answers:

- Width/length of treads — body/foot/leg width
- Diameter of ladder frame — grip diameter
- Vertical distance between treads — leg stretch
- Height of handrail — arm reach/stretch

Any suitable answer relating to human limitations, linking to part of the activity toy should be awarded one mark.

The use of physical action verbs linking to the use of the activity toy are to be looked for here, e.g. the activity toy has been designed to be moved easily by an adult around the garden.

Other suitable answers:

- The activity toy — moving, lifting, dragging, shifting
- Tread spacing — leg raise, climbing

Any suitable answer relating to human thoughts/feelings/emotions, linking to part or bit of the activity toy should be awarded one mark, e.g. the choice of bright/warm/advancing coloured material on the slide will ensure that the user knows which part is the fun part.

Other suitable answers:

- Bumpy appearance — fun/exciting
- Robust appearance — feeling of safety (for child/parent/carer)/stability
- Bright colours — fun

4. (a) • Models are used to develop an idea by giving a three dimensional view of a concept

- Models can be used to test for ergonomic and aesthetic decision making.

One mark per correct response up to total of two marks.

(b) Possible materials range from modelling clay through to wire, plywood, acrylic and smart modelling materials.

One mark awarded for the correct naming of each modelling material.

One mark should be awarded for suitable justification of each modelling material, e.g. modelling clay can be remoulded many times.

5. (a) (i) Note: environment here could mean either its working environment or its effect on the environment as a whole.

Description of environmental issues could include:
- Weather factors affecting its operation
- Properties of materials factors, corrosion etc
- Carbon footprint
- Awareness of potential fire risk to the local environment
- Ease of cleaning
- Ease of maintenance
- Any other reasonable response.

Any two described environmental issues for one mark each.

(ii) *Description of safety issues could include:*
- Safety of user
- Stability
- Safety to local environment
- Properties of materials relating to safety, heat, etc
- Hot surfaces
- Use of gas
- Any other reasonable response.

Any two described safety issues for one mark each.

(b) *Explanation should consider the following issues:*
- Identifying a need that is not being addressed by mainstream providers
- Narrowly defined group of potential customers
- Demand for a product that is not satisfactorily being met
- Small in comparison to the mainstream marketplace
- Specialization on small identifiable market areas
- Any other reasonable response

Any two explained issues for one mark each.

6. (a) • Primary functions versus secondary functions
   - Pocket tool — scissors and various functions. Original tools had one function — multi-tool has several
   - One main function plus additional uses or features

Two marks will be awarded for a described, clear answer.

(b) User trial, user trip, observation, user questionnaire

No marks for naming the technique, only for the description.

Two marks will be awarded for a described, clear answer.

(c) Shape of handles, curved lines, contrast in colours, logo stylish, plastic versus stainless steel, wow factor

Two marks will be awarded for a described, clear answer.

(d) Justified reason for stainless steel in context of this product strength/hardness/durability

One justified reason for one mark.

(e) Dip coat, powder coat, electro plating, spray painting

Two methods for one mark each.

7. (a) Morphological analysis, design stories

One mark per correct response up to a total of two marks

(b) **Design Stories:** to generate ideas using design stories you would put yourself in the place of the product you are designing. You would write a short story about a day in the life of the product or a story about the product being used. This then gives you a few ideas about what the product might need to do. This helps write the specification, which will lead to a range of ideas.

SECTION 1

1. (a) (i) Pine
   (ii) It can be locally sourced and it comes from sustainable forests.

(b) (i) The position of the peg would have been marked out by using a rule, pencil and try square. The rule would be used to measure along the edge of the piece of wood to the required dimension; this would be marked by the pencil. Then the try-square would be used with the pencil to mark lines at 90 degrees to the edge of the wood. This would then be measured and marked along to get the position of the peg.
   (ii) The peg would be joined to the box using PVA glue and a blind hole. The hole would be drilled using a hand drill or pillar drill.

(c) (i) Lap joint, dovetail joint
   (ii) **Lap joint:** after marking out the joint with a try square, marking gauge and rule, you would cut down halfway through the wood with a tenon saw. Then you would chisel out the waste wood with a bevel edged chisel. Finally you could use a hand router to smooth the bottom of the lap joint.
   (iii) **35mm hole:** after marking out with a rule and a try square, you would fit a forstener bit or flat bit to the pillar drill. You would then drill slowly through the wood to make sure you don't split it at the back.

(d) Varnish makes the box look good and it also makes it more durable and helps to protect the wood from rain and other weather conditions.

(e) Thermoplastic can be worked with and easily cut to size. It is also available in colours, such as green, which look good in an outdoors environment. It is also weatherproof and will not rot or fade in the outdoors.

(f) A wooden insert could be fitted to the inside of the roof which fits tightly into the internal space of the box. This would allow the roof to be lifted off easily and would add to the weight of the thermoplastic so it did not blow away.

SECTION 2

2. The designer would research: **Function**, **ergonomics**, **durability** and **safety**.

- **Function:** Function is important because the designer needs to find out what the docking station could do. Such as volume and tone settings for the music.
- **Ergonomics:** The buttons need to be easily pressed and fit human hand sizes.
- **Durability:** The materials used to make the docking station should withstand regular use, such as buttons or controls.
- **Safety:** The connections to the power source should be safe and not endanger the user from electric shock.

One mark for the four issues, and one mark for each explanation

3. (a) **The client:** Presentation drawing, pictorial drawings
   (b) **The manufacturer:** Orthographic drawing, exploded view
   (c) **Other designers:** Initial sketches, developed design details

4. (a) **Ease of use:** User trial — toast a piece of bread and describe how easy it was to use the toaster

 (b) **Aesthetics:** Survey — ask a group of people if they like the colour used in the design of the toaster

 (c) **Value for money:** Comparison to other products — compare the price of other products that do the same job and see if the toaster is a reasonable selling price

 (d) **Speed of toasting:** Testing — time the toaster to see how long it takes to toast the bread and compare to other toasters

5. (a) **Ergonomics:** Any relevant and true anthropometric, psychological or physiological explanation

 (b) **Safety:** Sharpness/bluntness/build quality/hygiene/weight/etc

 (c) **Aesthetics:** Shape/size/form/contrast/colour/encourage usage/etc

 (d) **Materials:** Comfortable/tactile/attractive or in-built colour/hygiene/safety/ease of cleaning/lightweight/non-allergenic/etc

6. (a) • Instant purchase
 • Easy to assemble
 • No delivery waiting
 • Low cost
 • Satisfaction of building
 • Easy to transport
 • Easy to store prior to assembly
 • Disassembly option, when not in use
 • Access to difficult property areas, such as up narrow staircases

 (b) • Low cost
 • Environmental reasons
 • Uniformity of thickness
 • Smooth surfaces
 • Easy to machine
 • Wide flat boards
 • Knock Down Fittings are compatible
 • Uses materials that might be considered as waste

 (c) • Special fittings to join furniture parts together
 • Mechanical fixing using standard components

 (d) A market niche is a particular group of people that a product could be aimed towards. Flat pack furniture is low cost and has a limited life span. Young families with less income would be the ideal market niche for flat pack furniture.

7. *Candidates have three possible routes to go down in their response: anthropometrics, physiology and psychology.*

 There is no requirement to refer to any of these areas by name. Typical responses within each aspect are shown below. Six suitable responses will gain six marks.

 Any suitable answer relating human dimensions and relevant aspect of the vacuum cleaner should be awarded one mark, e.g. the handle length has been designed to suit adult male 95th percentile palm width.

 Other suitable answers:
 • Trigger size — fingertip width
 • Gap between handle and main body — adult hand thickness

Any suitable answer relating to human limitations, linking to part of the activity toy should be awarded one mark.

The use of physical action verbs linking to the use of the vacuum cleaner are to be looked for here, e.g. the vacuum cleaner is lightweight so it can be moved easily by an adult around the house.

Other suitable answer:
The controls — easily turned/pressed/switched

Any suitable answer relating to human thoughts/feelings/emotions, linking to part or bit of the vacuum cleaner should be awarded one mark, e.g. the choice of white coloured material on the cleaner will make the user feel it is a hygienic product to use.

Other suitable answer:
Contrasting red and white — shows you where the uses can move or adjust and switch things

NATIONAL 5 DESIGN & MANUFACTURE MODEL PAPER 3

SECTION 1

1. (a) (i) Spruce
   (ii) They look modern and are environmentally friendly.

   (b) The cross halving joint would be marked out and then you could use a tenon saw to saw down halfway through the wood. A bevel edged chisel could then be used to remove the waste wood. This would be repeated on the other piece of wood. The two parts would then fit together making the halving joint.

   (c) A try-square, marking gauge, rule and pencil would be used to mark out the lap joint. The rule would be used to measure along the edge of the wood to the required dimension. The try-square would be used to mark the lines at 90 degrees to the edge and the marking gauge would be used to mark along the grain to join up with the try-square lines.

   (d) (i) Aluminium, brass
   (ii) The bar would be marked out using a rule, scriber and engineer's square. It could then be cut to size using a hacksaw.
   (iii) The bar would be put in an engineer's vice and filed smooth with a flat file. Emery cloth could then be used to smooth the filed surface.
   (iv) A 6mm hole could be drilled into the piece of wood on the pillar drill using a twist drill. Epoxy resin glue could then be used to permanently secure the metal in the hole.

   (e) The surfaces of wood would be sanded using sandpaper to remove pencil lines, excess glue and any dirty marks. The dust from sanding would then be removed using white spirit. The surfaces would then be ready for sanding.

   (f) Wax makes the unit look good and it also makes it more durable and helps to protect the wood from damage when items are placed onto it.

SECTION 2

2. The designer would research: **Function**, **ergonomics**, **durability** and **sustainability**.

   - **Function:** they would want to know what the main job of the grinders would be; would they need to be adjustable?
   - **Ergonomics:** they would need to know what sizes of the human body are important such as grip diameter.
   - **Durability:** they would need to know about different materials and what possible dangers they would need to withstand in a kitchen environment.
   - **Sustainability:** they would need to find out about the types of materials or woods that could be locally sourced and are sustainable to appeal to the environmentally aware customer.

   One mark for the four issues, one mark for each explanation.

3. (a) Consumers need to have a trainer that is fashionable and also comfortable to wear. This leads the manufacturers to make trainers that are both.

   (b) They could offer a special discount on gym membership if you buy a pair of trainers of that brand.

   They could give you a chance to win a trip to the next Olympics by asking you to phone a hotline with a code in your shoe box. This would increase sales.

4. (a) (i) The selling cost of the printer could be compared to other printers on the market and a decision could be made as to the value for money compared to the other printers.
   (ii) A survey could be carried out asking the public what their opinion of the colours used in the design of the printer. This could then lead to other colours being available.

   (b) CAD modelling is very quick and accurate and drawings can be altered very easily without a great deal of time being taken by the designer.

   (c) A model made out of resistant materials such as:
   - Styrofoam
   - A working drawing with dimensions
   - A final presentation drawing with the environment of the printer shown

5. (a) Morphological analysis, design stories
   One mark per correct response up to total of two marks.

   (b) **Morphological Analysis:** MA is a technique that you use to generate ideas by making columns of words from which you can pick random selections. The columns are under different headings like shape, colour and theme. This gives you a range of aspects to include in your idea.

6. (a) Rotational moulding
   (b) Turning
   (c) Sand Casting
   (d) Extrusion
   (e) Press-forming

7. Candidates have three possible routes to go down in their response: anthropometrics, physiology and psychology.

   There is no requirement to refer to any of these areas by name. Typical responses within each aspect are shown below. Six suitable responses will gain six marks.

   Any suitable answer relating human dimensions and relevant aspect of the hand held game should be awarded one mark, e.g. the buttons have been designed to suit children's finger tip sizes.

   Other suitable answer:
   Pointer diameter – child grip diameter

   Any suitable answer relating to human limitations, linking to part of the hand held game should be awarded one mark.

   The use of physical action verbs linking to the use of the hand held games are to be looked for here, e.g. the hand held game screen is easy for a child to open.

Other suitable answer:
The buttons — easily pressed

Any suitable answer relating to human thoughts/feelings/emotions, linking to part or bit of the hand held game should be awarded one mark, e.g. the choice of the pink coloured plastic makes it look like it is designed for girls.

Other suitable answer:
Contrasting and pink and white — show you where the controls to work the game are

NATIONAL 5 DESIGN & MANUFACTURE 2014

SECTION 1

1. (a) (i) *Any one from:*
   - cherry
   - mahogany
   - teak
   - walnut
   - oak
   - **Any other suitable response**

   (ii) *A description that covers two of the following:*
   - More variety of colours
   - Aesthetic ('looks good')
   - Durability
   - Better quality
   - Environmental
   - Strong
   - **Any other suitable response**

   (b) *Any two from:*
   - lap
   - corner rebate
   - mitre
   - dovetail
   - butt
   - dowel
   - biscuit joint
   - **Any other suitable response**

   (c) (i) *A description that covers two of the following benefits:*
   - Improves the appearance of the wood
   - Offers protection to the wood from bumps and scratches
   - Gives a waterproof surface
   - Gives a surface that can be easily wiped clean
   - Makes the wood more durable/hardwearing
   - **Any other suitable response**

   (ii) *A description that includes two of the following points:*
   - Remove pencil marks with eraser/sandpaper
   - Sand wood smooth
   - Dampen the wood to raise the grain
   - Sand wood again with smooth sand/glass/garnet/wet and dry paper
   - Steel wool (wirewool)
   - Remove dust / use white spirit / damp cloth
   - **Any other suitable response**

   (d) (i) *Explanations indicating that:*
   - Rounded corners prevent tearing of the plastic when it is being formed around the pattern

   (ii) *Explanations indicating that:*
   - Sloping sides allow the plastic to be removed easily from the pattern

   (iii) *Any two from:*
   - A plastic that has plastic memory/can be reformed if mistakes are made
   - Can be recycled
   - Available in a range of colours
   - Can easily be vacuum formed
   - Easy to clean
   - Cheap
   - Easy to work with
   - **Any other suitable response**

(e) (i) *A description that includes two of the following stages:*
- Fit the tool
- Fit the piece of work in the chuck
- Adjust compound slide to 45 degrees
- Move compound / cross slide to create chamfer
- **Any other suitable response**

(ii) *A description that includes two of the following:*
- Fit the cutting tool
- Fit the piece of work in the chuck
- Move tool to the start of the cut with the cross slide
- Reduce diameter with either compound slide or apron wheel
- **Any other suitable response**

(iii) *Any two from:*
- Depending on the diameter of the material
- Depending on the type of material
- Depending on the process being carried out (knurling/finishing)

(f) (i) *Any two from:*
- It has a relatively low melting temperature
- Lightweight
- Does not corrode
- Does not require finish
- Aesthetic reasons ('looks good')
- Strong
- Durable
- Non-ferrous
- Easy to work with
- **Any other suitable response**

(ii) *Any three from:*
- Can achieve intricate detail
- Mass production
- Speed of production
- Inexpensive
- Surface finish/looks good
- Components are identical
- **Any other suitable response**

SECTION 2

2. (a) **Anthropometrics**
To gain marks, the relationship between the ergonomic consideration and the part of the bicycle must be described.
Areas that may be covered:
- Saddle length/width
- Distance from saddle to peddles/saddle to handlebars
- Distance between handles
- Length/diameter of handles
- Distance from handles to brakes
- Length of brakes
- Width/length of pedal
- Length of gear trigger
- Adjustable parts, eg saddle
- Different frame sizes
- Weight of cyclist
- **Any other suitable response**

Physiology
Areas that may be covered:
- Strength required to pedal/pull brakes/change handlebar or saddle height/ turn handle bars & steer/ change gear
- **Any other suitable response**

Psychology
Areas that may be covered:
- Overall look – reference to intended market/safety/ease of use
- Sound from gear change/brakes/steering
- Feel of grips on handle bars/brakes/saddle
- Gear number indicators
- **Any other suitable response**

(b) (i) *Example response:*
- Durability would be researched because the user would expect the bike to last for several years without breaking or weakening.
- The designer would need to research which materials and joining methods would be strong enough to resist knocks and bumps and be able to be used in all kinds of weather.
- **Any other suitable response**

(ii) *Example response:*
- Ease of maintenance would be researched because a bike would have to be regularly maintained by the user in order to keep it in good working condition.
- The designer may have to investigate methods of changing or pumping up tyres, oiling chains and cleaning so they could then make the bike as easy as possible to keep working safely.
- **Any other suitable response**

(iii) *Example response:*
- Aesthetics would have to be researched so that the design team would have a good understanding of what fashions and trends the intended market is interested in.
- A bike for young girls would have a totally different look to a bike for teenage boys.
- **Any other suitable response**

3. *Candidates may make reference to:*
- Reduction in packaging
- Miniaturisation
- Recyclability
- Upcycling
- Number of parts/ease of separation of parts
- Services offered by brand – removal & recycling of old
- Energy use in production/in use
- Energy use in transportation
- Materials
- **Any other suitable response**

4. (a) (i) Possible Graphic techniques:
- Rough sketches
- Annotated sketches
- Perspective sketches
- 2D sketches
- 3D sketches
- Sketches
- Roughs
- **Any other suitable response**

Example response:
A designer may use annotated sketches at the initial ideas stage because it is a quick technique, allowing them to sketch out various ideas and note their thoughts next to them.

(ii) Possible Graphic techniques:
- Working drawing
- Exploded views
- Assemblies
- Sections
- 3D solid CAD model

- Storyboard
- **Any other suitable response**

Example responses:
A working drawing would be used at the planning for manufacture stage as the design team would need to note down the accurate dimensions of the product.
The assembly drawing will help the team understand what it looks like and how the components fit together.

(b) Modelling Materials:
- Paper
- Card
- Corrugated Card
- MDF
- Wire
- Pipe Cleaners
- Foam
- Clay
- Modelling compound
- Balsa Wood
- Expanded Foam
- Sheet Plastic
- Construction kit
- Wood
- **Any other suitable response**

Example responses:
Corrugated card is a good material for modelling as it can be easily joined with masking tape. (2 marks)
Designers use clay because it can be easily shaped with your hands and can be made into unusual shapes that can't be made with sheet material. (2 marks)

5. (a) (i) • Water/rust resistant
- Tasteless
- Aesthetics – modern look/ matches other appliances
- Easy to clean
- Hygienic
- Resists chemical cleaners
- Ergonomic reasons
- Link to manufacturing process – available in sheet form
- Strong/hardwearing/robust
- Heavy (for stability during use)
- **Any other suitable response**

(ii) • Speed of production
- Economies of scale/cheaper
- Component accuracy
- Quality of finish
- Uniformity
- Reduced workforce
- **Any other suitable response**

(b) Injection moulding

(c) • Cost of equipment/machinery
- Cost to maintain equipment/machinery
- Cost of staff training
- Time for staff training/re-training
- Impact on environment of new equipment/ machinery
- Disposal of old equipment/ machinery
- Can stay ahead of the competition/adapt designs/ new designs
- Allow new shapes/less joining techniques to be used
- Reduce unit cost
- Reduce labour costs

- Reduce material used
- Quicker production methods
- More accurate production methods
- Can facilitate rapid prototyping
- **Any other suitable response**

6. (a) *Example responses:*
Users could press the button to switch the razor on and off. They could then comment on ease of use. (2 marks)
The users could hold the razor and comment on how comfortable it is to hold. (2 marks)

(b) *Example responses:*
Comment on the shape of the razor.
Rate the colour of the razor on a scale of 1 to 10, 10 being the best.

(c) Possible answers:
- Eye-catching packaging
- Reduced or lower price point/ introductory offer
- Promotional offers – BOGOF/ free shaving gel
- Sell under a brand name
- Adapt to suit a new market segment
- Celebrity endorsement
- Specific advertising techniques
- **Any other suitable response**

Example responses:
A design team may decide to reduce the price of the razor when it enters onto the market. (1 mark)
A design team may get people interested in buying their products by offering an additional product, for example free shaving gel or moisturiser. (1 mark)

(d) Candidates must describe one of the following to gain full marks:
- Morphological Analysis
- Brain storming
- Technology Transfer
- Analogy
- Lateral Thinking
- Mood board
- Lifestyle board
- Take your pencil for a walk
- Design Stories
- Gathering public opinion through a market survey
- **Any other suitable response**

Example answer:
Brain storming
The team will sit together and note down all of the ideas each person has, no matter how silly they seem. Some ideas may spark off thoughts in others, allowing different suggestions to be explored in the hope of coming up with a new idea.

Acknowledgements

Permission has been sought from all relevant copyright holders and Hodder Gibson is grateful for the use of the following:

The Perspex ® Trademark © Lucite International (SQP page 6);
Image © ppart/Shutterstock.com (SQP page 7);
Image © Plus69/Shutterstock.com (SQP page 7);
Image © forest_strider/Shutterstock.com (SQP page 9);
Image © Mr. Aesthetics/Shutterstock.com (SQP page 9);
Image © Jeremy Smith/Shutterstock.com (SQP page 9);
Image © photosync/Shutterstock.com (SQP page 12);
Image © Peter Polak/Shutterstock.com (SQP page 13);
Image © Madlen/Shutterstock.com (SQP page 13);
Image © DenisNata/Shutterstock.com (SQP page 13);
Image © George Dolgikh/Shutterstock.com (SQP page 14);
Image © nexus 7/Shutterstock.com (SQP page 14);
Photo of a BenQ computer mouse © BenQ Europe B.V. (Model Paper 1 page 5);
Fotolia 37832391: © photoshaker-Fotolia (Model Paper 1 page 7);
Photo of a Gerber multi-tool © Silva Ltd (Model Paper 1 page 8);
Photo of an intempo iPod docking station © Intempo, Ultimate Products Ltd. (Model Paper 2 page 5);
Photo of a Dualit toaster © Dualit Ltd (Model Paper 2 page 6);
Photo of a Black & Decker DustBuster CHV1500 © Black & Decker (Model Paper 2 page 9);
Fotolia 44425162: gleebpl-Fotolia (Model Paper 3 page 6);
Fotolia 13293392: © Tatesh-Fotolia (Model Paper 3 page 6);
Fotolia 49526034: © Tomasz Zajda-Fotolia (Model Paper 3 page 6);
Fotolia 3253692: © Alex-Fotolia (Model Paper 3 page 7);
HRF 4222788: © istockphoto/Greg Nicholas (Model Paper 3 page 8);
Photo of a Nintendo DS © Nintendo UK (Model Paper 3 page 11);
Image © RAJ CREATIONZS/Shutterstock.com (2014 page 5);
Image © Cameron Spencer/Getty Images (2014 page 6);
Image © Quinn Rooney/Getty Images (2014 page 6);
Image © Bryn Lennon/Getty Images (2014 page 6);
Image © Dawes Cycles (2014 page 6);
Image © Alina Ku-Ku/Shutterstock.com (2014 page 8);
Image © rtguest/Shutterstock.com (2014 page 8);
Image © FEV/Shutterstock.com (2014 page 9);
Image © Wth/Shutterstock.com (2014 page 9);
Image © Gavran333/Shutterstock.com (2014 page 11);
Image © Africa Studio/Shutterstock.com (2014 page 11);
Image © Sandra van der Steen/Shutterstock.com (2014 page 12);
Image © Simon Krzic/Shutterstock.com (2014 page 12);
Image © Mehmet Dilsiz/Shutterstock.com (2014 page 13);
Image © Art Konovalov/Shutterstock.com (2014 page 14);
Image © Nixx Photography/Shutterstock.com (2014 page 14);
Image © Pakhnyushcha/Shutterstock.com (2014 page 14).

Hodder Gibson would like to thank SQA for use of any past exam questions that may have been used in model papers, whether amended or in original form.